To : Orsia
Only by .
mit -
Sarah

Only by His Grace

Sarah Berthelson

PRESS

10/09

I dedicate this book
In loving memory of my son
Ky Adam Berthelson
October 5, 1965-July 25, 1994
To his birthmother
Jeanne Lidwell and her family
Dan, Kacei, Kelli, and Blair
And to the wonderful men in my life
George, Chad and Shay
Thank you

Forward

It is a joy to see how God is using Sarah to speak through this book to be an encourager and share the faith God gave her to walk through the trials, heartaches, and doubts in her life.

I count it a privilege to have been her pastor for the past 28 years and to walk with her and her husband George in their journey of faith of our Lord and Savior Jesus Christ. I want to thank you Sarah, for being available to let the Lord use you to help so many people who need encouragement and strength in their lives.

Your Pastor,

Ray Newcomb

Dr. Ray Newcomb
Pastor First Baptist Church
Millington, Tennessee

Introduction

Only by God's grace, I am writing another book. This is my third book and I am writing more about my story after many dear friends from around the world have asked me to do so. I am thankful God has given me the opportunity to share my love for my Lord Jesus Christ and the guidance he has given me through the years. My college English professor has gone to be with the Lord but I am sure I am the last of his students that he would have guessed to write a book or a poem. I am as surprised as he would be. This book came about after the birth mother of my first child came back into my life. God is an awesome God and I never realized what a plan he had for my life until He showed me one day at a time. This book has some old fashion spiritual wisdom added to it. Hopefully, parents, grandparents and young people will read it and allow God to speak to them through this book. May you be blessed as you read this story about me and my family as we have attempted to serve our Lord faithfully.

Hebrews 4:12 *For the word of God is quick, and powerful, and sharper than any two edged sword, piercing even to the dividing asunder of soul and spirit, and of joints and marrow, and is a discerner of the thoughts and intents of the heart.*

Only By His Grace

Only by my wonderful Savior's grace,
I am at peace and happy in this place.

There has been heartache, sickness, and death
in my world - that I have experienced this year.

Only by His grace can I sing and laugh today.
He is always listening and answering as I pray.

He did not promise that all would be contentment.
That is the reason I feel His presence
and have no resentment.

There should be no bitterness when
things go wrong.
He should not get blamed for all the times
I am not strong.

How often I blame God for the situation I am in.
It is not His fault that I have chosen to sin.

Only by His wonderful grace,
I have the peace within.
I am so thankful that He was with me
through it all.

He touched my brow with His tender touch.
When I needed him the most,
He let me know He loved me so very much.

Only by His grace I can sit and write.
Only by His grace I have my sight.

Chapter 1

Yesterday Living

My parents were wonderful Christians and they loved their family with all their hearts. They taught us about Jesus Christ as youngsters and took us to church. I loved going to church. Not only was it a place of peace, worship and fellowship but it was my only social outing as a child. I loved it when my mother invited the preacher for Sunday dinner. There were times that she invited almost everyone in the church. I remember certain families that would always be there. One was the principle of our High School, Mr. Simmons, and his family. I thought it was cool that he came to our house and was such good friends with my dad.

We always had so much good food and plenty of fried chicken. I can remember Mama and Daddy wringing the neck of the chicken. Then they put the chicken into hot water and pulled all the feathers off. Now, for a kid that lived way down an old road out in the country, that was entertainment! Not many people came down that road unless it was the mailman, grocery man or someone going to see our neighbors that lived across the creek. I would sit on the porch in the summer time and watch for someone to just pass by. The country life and having Christian parents were things I took for granted. We can not turn back the clock on time but those truly were the good old days. I was so innocent of drugs, sex and the things that are going on today. We also left our doors and windows open. The thought that someone would come into our home uninvited never crossed our minds. If anyone had walked in while we were in the fields or gone to town, they would not have taken anything. People were honest and as good as their word. A hand shake was all that Daddy needed to seal a deal. People believed in and trusted one another. I know there were bad people in the world but not in my world. How thankful I am for the way I grew up. There was not much money but there was a whole lot of love and fun times. We played with whatever we could find. I remember my brother making a baseball out of an old sock. I have no idea what he put in it but it was a baseball and he could play baseball with it. In the summer time we could go swimming anytime we wanted to. We did not have a fancy swimming pool but we had a creek that flowed with clear, wonderful, cool water. If we did not want to swim in the one by our house we had several options of others. Many Sunday afternoons, half the church kids would go swimming in that old creek or we would go to the Fugler's place where we could dive off the bank and swim there. That was how swimming was done in the olden days, as the kids today like to call them. We were not under-privileged by any means, all the kids in the community were raised alike.

Nowadays, everyone seems interested in their clothes. There is so much fashion today. Models are strutting around showing off what is going to be the "in" thing for the season. Well, we didn't worry about that stuff. Those fashions do not look good on everyone. I believe that every child should be raised with a full length mirror close by so they can see what they look like before walking out the door. I would imagine some of them would go back and change their clothes.

When I was very young and Daddy was farming, feed sacks came in beautiful colors and floral patterns. Mama would wash those sacks and take them to my Aunt Lou or Aunt Jessie, the ones who could sew, and they would make me a beautiful dress or skirt. Now, you might think I was pretty needy, but I really was not. My parents saw to it that I had nice cloths as I was growing up. My parents dressed nicely and my mother loved to wear her hat to church on Sunday. We dressed in our very best to go to Church. Then we came home and put on our old clothes for play.

All my family picked cotton but I will have to admit that I did not. Being the baby had its advantages. I can remember when my mother learned to raise chrysanthemums, which are beautiful flowers. They were very time consuming but in February she would sell them to a florist. Mainly in New Orleans which was only about one hundred and twenty miles away. She made a lot of money for the season.

Proverbs 31: 30 *Favor is deceitful, and beauty is vain: but a woman that feareth the Lord, she shall be praised.*

When I was very young, we lived in my grandfather's old home. My Mother and Daddy took care of him until his death. We lived there several years, and then my brother Dewey, who worked for the Public Service in New Orleans, bought a home in our area and deeded it to my parents until their death. Not many children would do what my brother did for us. My older sisters and brothers had graduated from High School and gone their separate ways. I had my own room and loved living in that house. I did not have to change schools since my dad drove the school bus that I rode to school. My parents and I did move our church membership to nearby Wellman Baptist Church. I had the best of two worlds, or so I thought. I had friends at Wellman church that went to Enterprise School and I went to school at Fair Oak Springs, so I had lots of wonderful friends in my High School years. I lived in a loving and safe environment. My parents were getting older and they had already raised four children. They needed to slow down a bit with me. They attended the programs I was involved in at school and church but did not go with me just to be going somewhere. I rode to church on Sunday nights with one of our neighbors. My parents did not miss the revivals though. One of the things that I remember most about them in my teen years was our doors were always open for my friends and social activities. We had many youth parties at our home. My daddy was funny and always played tricks on the other kids. Sometimes he would scare them half to death with some of his pranks but it was all in fun. My dad had a contagious laugh and could have a group of kids laughing their heads off, everyone except the one the trick was played on. I never knew anyone that did not love Mr. Lemmie. That was my dad and I was so very proud of him.

I wanted to be a teacher all my life. So when I graduated from High School, I went to college and got my degree in Elementary Education. My first teaching job was in Meridian, Mississippi at Highland School, where I taught fifth grade. I loved teaching and every student that was sent into my class. I gave the most attention to the ones that had the most difficulty in their lives. I shared that Jesus Christ was my personal Lord and savior with my class. They knew that I loved Him and wanted to serve Him. I wanted them to know Him as I did. I have gotten emails and letters from some of those fifth graders, who are now grandparents; just to tell me how much I meant to them as their fifth grade teacher. Tears flow down my face when I hear from those that I seem to have made a difference in their life. It saddens me to know that my grandchildren cannot share their faith with their classmates. The teachers cannot tell them about Jesus and how He and only He can help them through the difficult time they will face in this life. I understand that times have changed and many changes needed to have taken place.

I am not against anyone believing whatever they want to believe but for me, I believe that Jesus Christ was born of a virgin, was crucified, buried in a tomb and was raised from the dead on the third day. I believe every word of the Bible to be true.

I believe John 3:16 *For God so loved the world, that He gave His only begotten Son, that whosoever believeth on Him should not perish, but have everlasting life.*

I believe that because of God's sacrifice that everyone that accepts Jesus Christ will go to heaven when they die. That is exactly what I believe and hope you do also. Just read God's word and that is what it teaches. So many people take the Bible and have it say whatever they want it to say. They will argue their point. I do not argue but I know what I believe and who I believe in. I just want people to love the Lord Jesus and each other as God loves us.

While in Meridian, I met the love of my life. A friend and I were at a drive-in one night getting our Coke and Fritos when three young men drove up beside us. One of them decided to talk to us. We were not really interested but enjoyed talking to him. The other two acted as if we did not exist. The one we met called the next day and wanted to know if he and a friend could come over. It was a Saturday, so we did not care. That day changed my life. The young man that came with him was a Christian from Montana and was undergoing flight training at the base. The four of us went to the drive-in for a Coke, just to go for a ride. I ended up sitting in the back seat with this young man from Montana. He was handsome but I certainly wasn't interested in him. I didn't think he was interested in me either. Well guess what, he was. He began to pursue me with phone calls every day. He could not come in from the base so he would just call and talk forever. He also wrote me a letter every week, a very long letter and had it sent to my school. My principal enjoyed that part of our courtship. When she received the letter she would call me to the office. Well, I was embarrassed a little bit. George and I would go to a movie on Saturday night or out to eat. Sunday, we went to church. I was very involved in Calvary Baptist Church. I was teaching the senior girls in Sunday school. They were such a joy, since I was not too much older than they were. In fact, one became a very good friend to me.

After four months of dating and then meeting my family, he asked me to marry him. He is the first boy I had taken to meet them that they all approved of. My Mother fell in love with him before I did. So did my sister Mary. Boy, was that a plus for him. I thought he was crazy as could be to be talking marriage. He was a cadet and was not suppose to get married until he finished flight training. I wrote my preacher brother, Wiley, to call me so I could ask him if he would marry us. He called and he said that he would meet us any where we wanted him to and he would perform the ceremony. I have never been more nervous. I told George that I could not get married without telling my wonderful parents. He agreed to that. Then I told him I couldn't get married without my brother Dewey and his wife, Elnor; my sister Mary and brother-in-law, Don; and then my sister Billie and her husband, George. Before I was through, he was a little frustrated with this girl that he thought he could not live without. She had invited her entire family to this secret wedding.

We were married February 17, 1962 in my parent's living room, with my family there. He wore his uniform and I wore a suit that I could barely afford on my teachers salary. We were late for our wedding since his Commanding Officer scheduled him for a flight that Saturday morning. So I waited and waited until he arrived to pick me up about noon.

Contemplating this crazy thing that I was about to do, I did a lot of praying. I had not met his family and Southern girls have to meet the groom's family before they marry, so I thought. Instead of marrying in the afternoon as we had planned, it was 7:00 that evening. He had to be back at the base Sunday evening but I wasn't finished telling folks yet. We went by Canton, Mississippi so I could tell my best friend, Marolyn Weems. On Monday morning, this new bride had to go to school and teach her fifth graders, but not before I stopped by the principals office and told my wonderful friend Miss Stribling that I was married and proudly displayed my wedding band that I was wearing on a chain around my neck (it wasn't showing). I had left out one of the most special people in Meridian to me and that was my pastor, Dr. Seal. I went that Monday afternoon and told him. Everyone was very happy for me. They had met George and liked him and they kept our secret. In April, George bought me a beautiful engagement ring. I am not sure that is what you would have called it but I could proudly display the fact that I was taken. I loved my husband. He had gone back to Pensacola and I finished teaching that school year at Meridian. When George finished up at Pensacola, he went to Kingsville, Texas, to finish up his training. Once he was finished, we could finally tell the world that we were married. After I finished the school year, my parents took me to catch the train from Brookhaven to Texas, where George had gotten an apartment for me. No, he still could not live there. I will never forget what my wise Daddy said to me, "Baby you belong to George now, so you go and make him a good wife." I have done my best—well, I suppose it is my best. I lived in an apartment and did not see George except on week-ends. Many week-ends, he had to take a cross country flight and I was there alone then, too. Well, I wasn't really alone and I wasn't afraid. I relied on my faith in the Lord Jesus and I knew He was there with me. I could not make friends for fear they would find out about our marriage and tell the military on us. I did know my landlady and her husband but that was okay. They had no clue why George did not stay with me. They were senior citizens and just knew he was a Marine and was working. He came home when he could. I think I would have been a little bit more inquisitive than they were.

When George received his wings, I had the honor of pinning them on his chest. I was very happy to do so, that meant we were free to be a married couple. Then we left to go to Montana for me to meet his family. I had never been out West and George's daddy became my hero of the West. I wrote this poem about him.

My Very Own Cowboy

When I was growing up, I went to the movies on
Saturday afternoon to see the cowboys
on the screen

I was in love with Roy Rogers, Gene Autry
and Lash LaRue and never knew what
a real cowboy was

The one on the screen was handsome and
all the Southern girls like me
couldn't wait until the next Saturday
so we could watch them again

I didn't know what a range was; I just knew that
I would like to see one

The cowboys rode their horses and rounded up
cattle, often killing the bad guy too

Well I met a real live cowboy in 1962, he was
everything I dreamed that a
Cowboy would be

He was tall, dark and handsome, and could tell a
tale that you could believe

I was smitten by him and it only took a few
minutes to realize
this is just like the guy on the big screen, how
excited could this Southern girl be

He put his long arms around me and welcomed me
in, laughed at my accent
and gave me a grin

This wonderful man that I met in Montana, was the
hunk that was called Ken

He never met a stranger, he made everyone laugh,

Ken Berthelson was my father-in-law and you
cannot beat that

I was so proud to be in his presence and to be
introduced as his kin

There never was but one and never will be another,
Montana Cowboy like my father-in-law KEN!!!!

This secret marriage was absolutely insane, on my part. I had dreamed of the white dress and veil just like all little girls. But who can beat a story like this and it is absolutely true.

Chapter 2

We Wanted a Baby

Proverbs 3:5-6 *Trust in the Lord with all thine heart and lean not unto thine own understanding. In all thy ways acknowledge him and he shall direct thy path.*

Forty-two years ago, my husband and I had the wonderful privilege of adopting our first child. I had been told I could not have children for medical reasons. We had prayed and asked God to show us what He would have us to do. We did not know much about the adoption process, or even how to start to apply. After much prayer we felt led to go to an adoption agency in the county where we lived. We went through the adoption process. Our home was set up and we were very happy to hear that we would get a baby soon. As the military would have it, my husband received orders to another base in the same state but a different county. We never thought there would be a problem with the adoption process but that was not the case. We were told we would have to start the entire process all over again in the new county. There was a back-log of adoption cases that was 2 years in the arrears and we knew we would only be there 1 year. The discouragement was overwhelming. It all seemed just too much to bear.

Soon afterwards, my husband received orders to go to Cuba for three months. He did not want to leave me at the base since I had family in Mississippi. I am the youngest of five siblings so I wanted to go to my mama and daddy. I was saddened by the fact that my husband was leaving and that I could not look forward to getting a baby.

There is a lot of pain as we go through this old world but God's grace is sufficient regardless of what we are going through. He has placed loved ones and friends in my life to help ease the pains of life. More than anything I could feel my Lord's presence regardless of what was causing my pain.

I knew that I would be happier being with my family instead of staying at Camp Lejeune, North Carolina. George went to Cuba and I went to Mississippi to spend that time with my parents who lived in the country, six miles from Brookhaven. My friends and family knew how much I wanted a child. I had prayed and begged God to show me what to do. I never saw what He had in mind for George and me.

Mama, Daddy and I were sitting on the porch when the phone rang and it was my sister, Billie. She worked for the telephone company in New Orleans. After a coffee break she was returning to work when she told some friend that she would love it if her sister and brother-in-law could get a baby. The next day one of her friends brought her a telephone number. It was for her neighbor's niece who lived in Everett, Washington and was only seventeen years old and pregnant.

I called this young lady, Jeanne, and told her who I was and asked her if she would be willing to come to Brookhaven and let George and I adopt her baby. This story is in more detail in He Guides My Path, the first book that I wrote. Well, to my surprise and excitement she said she would gladly come. Now here I was in a far away state, with this long southern drawl, asking this child from the Northwest to come and live with me and give me the baby she was carrying. This was God's amazing grace bringing the two of us together. I wanted a baby more than anything and she needed someone to adopt the baby she was carrying. Forty years ago unwed mothers did not keep the babies as much as they do now. She came to live with my parents and me. We got to know each other well and I loved her.

God, to my amazement, allowed me to present the plan of salvation to Jeanne at my parent's table the second night she was there. She accepted Jesus as her Lord and savior. I bought her a Bible. She was not raised in a Christian home as I was. She was baptized in the little country church where I worshipped in my teenage years. Jeanne was one of the most beautiful young ladies I had ever met. She was vivacious and loved everyone in my family and they loved her. What a wonderful experience God gave us.

George and I decided to name our son Ky Adam Berthelson. I wanted him to have his grandfather's initials. I could not think of a name with the initials K. A. that I liked. I really liked the name Ken but half the Berthelson men were named Ken. My aunt Mattie who lived in Louisiana told me to name him Ky. She and Mama had an uncle named Hezekiah but he was called Ky. We were not sure how to spell it, but thought that was a good name for our baby. Since he was my first born, Adam seemed appropriate for a middle name. Jeanne knew what we named him.

George came home from Cuba and I went back to North Carolina with him, six weeks before Ky's birth. I had accepted a teaching position there before we knew we were getting a baby. I went back to teach and get things in order before Ky's birth in October. Jeanne stayed with my sister and brother-in-law, Mary and Don, the last few weeks before Ky was born. They lived in Brookhaven near the hospital.

On October 5, 1965, Mary called and said "you have a baby boy!" I was so excited that I could not think straight but I had enough sense to call George and tell him. He immediately asked for leave from work and came to get me.

We had bought my daddy a second-hand car so we planned to tow it with our van. Oh my goodness, we drove in the worst rain storm I have ever been in. The rain came down and the wind nearly blew us off the highway so many times. The car we were pulling would go one way and the van the other. Needless to say, that was not a pleasant trip. God's amazing grace got us to Brookhaven without an accident or a delay. Dr. Wilkins who delivered Ky would not allow anyone to see the baby until we arrived.

After twelve hours of being rained on and blown around, we arrived at the hospital. The nurse opened the curtain to the nursery and rolled that little basket up to the window. I burst into tears. There lay my beautiful baby boy. He was all red except for a little black hair, and all his parts were intact. I went to Jeanne's room and their lay that beautiful, black-haired young lady that had given me this wonderful gift. She looked at me and saw the tears and said "Oh, you don't like him"! I hugged her and said, "Oh, Yes I do! I love him!".

When the baby was five days old, we adopted him and Jeanne started on her way back home. I remember shedding tears when she left. She never saw my beautiful son, Ky. We thought it was best for her not to see his face. Jeanne agreed that she could never get his face off her mind. She was so

31

young and could not take care of a child. She did not choose abortion and for that I am so thankful. God in His divine wisdom closed all the doors on our prior attempts to adopt so we could have this special child that He had for us. I never thought I would see Jeanne again and that broke my heart.

We stayed in Brookhaven for several days so my family could meet the new addition to our family. We then went to North Carolina where I was teaching but I resigned immediately. I wanted to stay home and take care of my baby. I had to finish up two weeks before I could stop teaching. A dear lady from our church took care of Ky while I was teaching. I could not concentrate on teaching, at all. All I could think of was picking up my baby from her house and going home to George. We loved being parents. George gave Ky his bath in a little blue tub many nights just to be near him. I would watch with a smile on my face. Now isn't God good? Only by His grace did we have this child.

Matthew 21:22 *And all things, whatsoever ye shall ask in prayer, believing, ye shall receive.*

Chapter 3

This Can't Be

Matthew 6:8 *Your Father knoweth what things ye have need of, before ye ask him.*

Ky was six months old when I became very ill. I went to the doctor and he told me I was pregnant. I told him I wasn't because I could not get pregnant. He was a nice military doctor and did not argue my point but I remember a smile. Yes, you guessed it. Our Chad was born January 13, 1967, when Ky was only fifteen months old. He was so beautiful and I was so proud that I had experienced this wonderful thing called "giving birth". It was not fun. My mother told me that I would forget the pain. Well, Chad is forty years old and I still remember the pain. I chose Chad's name after watching Chad Everett on television. Later on, he became very famous when he played Dr. Joe Gannon in "Medical

Center". Anyway, he was handsome. I did a good job because my Chad is handsome. George was in Vietnam and did not meet his son until he was eleven months old. That was an experience many military wives go through and it is not enjoyable. You want your husband there more than anyone. Well, mine wasn't there. Am I bitter? If I even thought of bitterness, God got even. Three years later George received orders to go back to Vietnam. Well, I got sick again. Only a week before he left I thought I had a bad case of nerves. George said, "You are going to the doctor before I leave". Dr. Wilkins met us at his office on Sunday afternoon before George left on Monday. Oh yes, I was pregnant. I thought to myself I cannot do this again. You know what? I did and I had a beautiful baby boy, Shay, January 23, 1971. I just knew I was going to have a girl this time, so I didn't even think much about boy's names. My sister Mary came home from church just before Shay was born and told me she had the cutest little boy in her two year old class whose name was Shay. Since I wanted short names to go with this long last name, Shay sounded wonderful. I did not know a Shay. Only by His grace that Dr. Wilkins a surgeon delivered all three of my sons. Now being in the military that just doesn't happen. He kept his boys (as he called them) pictures on his desk until he retired. Shay was three months old when his dad met him and soon after that, our family moved to Beaufort, South Carolina.

You Are My Hero

My guy was a marine and I was so proud.
One day, he came home to say
'To Vietnam I am to go'. I cried out loud,
Looking at my one year old little boy.

In two months, I gave birth to a second son.
My hero was flying his airplane across the sky
when our son was born. I just had to cry.
His dad would not see him for another year.

He came home to me and two little boys,
holding his head down because,
Back then, he did not feel proud.
He was not supported for all that he did.

So many were against that war.
Some shouted and screamed that he should
not be there,
Three years later, he came home to say
'I will go back to Vietnam'.

Again, my heart broke for the sadness and fear.
I thought 'another year I must endure'.
Seven months and I was to give birth to
our third son.
Again, in the maternity ward, I felt so alone.

My hero came home and I was so proud.
Yet, no one clapped as he got off the plane.
No one said, "Thank you, Marine,
for your sacrifice."
He did not ask to go and fight but he did proudly

He was not there for the birth of either son.
He was fighting a war for them to be free.
He is my hero, you see.

GOD BLESS OUR TROOPS

1 Thessalonians 5:18 *In every thing give thanks: for this is the will of God in Christ Jesus concerning you.*

Chapter 4

Raising Children

Ephesians 6:1-3 *Children, obey your parents in the lord: for this is right. Honor thy father and mother; which is the first commandment with promise; that it may be well with thee, and thou mayest live long on the earth.*

K y started the first grade in Beaufort. The next year, when he was in second grade, Chad was in Kindergarten and I had my baby, Shay, to take care of at home. Only by his grace did these great things happen in my life. His grace took care of all the tears I had shed from doctors telling me I could not have a child and the disappointments with the adoption agencies. Through it all, George and I kept our faith and were willing to go through life childless if that was God's will. I know there are many couples wondering why they cannot have a child. I do not know why this happens but I do know that you must give the desires of your heart to the Lord. He can work miracles as He did in our life. We had a family.

It was so much fun raising our sons. Chad and Ky were close in age so they did many things together. We got involved in a church right away when we had to move for the military. They knew Jesus at a young age and accepted him. Chad at age six, was at a backyard Bible study in Beaufort when he came running home as fast as his little legs would carry him to tell me he had asked Jesus into his heart. I have never doubted that for a moment. He has the gift of prophecy and I have never doubted that, once I studied the gifts. I think parents need to know their children's spiritual gift. There is no in-between with Chad; everything is either right or wrong. He makes me smile with his gift. Since I have the gift of mercy, I try to understand. That is, with a smile. Ky accepted the Lord on his tenth birthday at Brighton Baptist Church in Brighton, Tennessee. I am not sure what his motivational gift was, but I know he loved to help people and was very patient with children. He had a heart for the mentally or physically challenged. My Shay wanted to be baptized in Okinawa so at 6 he told me he had invited Jesus in his heart and was baptized. When he became a teenager he told me that he did not think he was saved, we all think this at one time or the other. He went forward and was baptized at Millington First Baptist. Shay has the gift of exhortation. I know because he lifts his mama up when she is down. He can tell by my voice on the phone if I am doing well or not. He loves people and has a desire to help in anyway he can. He is a very positive person and can help those that are discouraged.

When parents know what motivates their children to do what they do for the Lord Jesus Christ, it helps to understand them better. Thankfully, we don't all have the same gift. That is the reason we react to situations differently. I will cry over a dead bird, while my family reacts very differently. My George has the gift of service and he will help anyone do anything at anytime. Parents need to share Bible verses with their children that will go along with whatever is on their heart. I pray for children that never get to know what it is like to go to church camp or be in a Sunday school class. How sad that they miss this wonderful experience as they grow up. My boys learned more Bible verses at Church camp than any other time. What a blessing to have God's word instilled in their hearts.

There have never been two people more pleased to have children than my George and I. It was not always easy but it was great. The hardest thing we encountered was that these little people did not come with directions. The only help I got was from my own growing up experiences and Dr. Spock. I don't think his book is popular anymore. He helped me out in many a crises. Especially in the middle of the night if one had an ear ache or got sick. I could not run to the emergency room every time one was sick. I ran to get my Dr. Spock book to see what page I should look on for a specific problem. My mother wasn't there to tell me what to do either. I was on my own; it was God, Dr. Spock and me. I knew I could do this. My priority was taking care of my little boys. There were times two would be sick at once. That was not fun and I sure did not get a lot of sleep. I thought that Dr. Spock' book was great.. Not many of our young people have heard of him. Like they do not know what a cloth diaper is. Well, I didn't know what a pamper was. What a benefit that would have been for all the military wives with children. We had to travel so much and would hunt for a washateria. That is where you had to find a coin operated washing machine and dryer. Now are you spoiled or what?

One of the benefits of being a military family was we had great health benefits which came in handy. Chad was our accident prone child. He was also the one with constant ear infections and sinus problems. He was often in the emergency room. He was the explorer that always got into more than he could handle. He went to pick up sea shell one day not far from our base house at Beaufort and cut his hand badly on a sea shell and away we went for stitches. As he remembers it we then went to a movie and he was in terrible agony. That is what inexperienced parents often face. Actually we thought the movie would take his mind off his pain. Chad will tell you very quickly that it did not. A lesson learned for these parents.

There are many stories about Chad and accidents plus he was the one that it seemed that dogs could smell a mile away and they liked to bite him. Poor child had some difficult times in his childhood. Now he is a wonderful father of three. He has all these memories to fall back on. We don't always see eye to eye on the way he remembers things. I am sure that some of you have grown kids like that.

I tried to spend quality time with each boy but it was hard to do at times. That is the one regret that I have as a mother. Chad and Ky were doing things at the same time. Ky was the one that I spoiled the most, according to Chad. Since Ky was adopted I never wanted him to think that I loved Chad and Shay more so I compensated by over-doing for him.

If he wanted a new pair of shoes because another kid at school had some, then I would go get them. Chad got a pair also but he will not admit that today. Ky was a good boy and enjoyed being spoiled. He played games with us by using that at times. It would not take long for George and me to catch on to what he was doing. Oh well, I just told you they didn't come with instructions. Now Shay, the baby, was spoiled also and got away with more than the other two. As you know by the time the third one comes along you are really experienced so you just let them go. We lived only about three blocks from the swimming pool on base. He was only in the second grade and I would let him go to the pool for the day. He was a water baby before we knew the term. He could barely walk when we noticed that he would be in the kid's pool while the other two were in the big pool with their dad. Shay would go under water and pick up pennies. Oh we thought he was a water genius. He loved to swim and we let him. We never thought of danger like we have to do today with children. The life guards at the pool would watch after him. They would stamp his hand so he could come and eat or get a snack and away he would go back to the pool. The pool was my baby sitter in the summer.

Young couples make sure you are spending quality time with your precious children. You blink and they will be gone. Show them respect and love and they will show you the same.

My Children have been taught right from wrong. They are teaching their children the same principles. Are they perfect and will their children be perfect? Absolutely not, but their conscience goes into effect when they do wrong just as mine did. I never wanted to hurt the ones I loved and that taught me to be a good person. I believe when we teach our children Biblical principles they will try to live by them. I see many parents today that are living a life that is pleasing to our Lord Jesus and they are teaching their children by example how to live a Christian life.

My heart goes out to single parents but you can do this and do a good job. Just put Jesus Christ first place in your heart and your home and He will help you on a day to day basis. There are many well adjusted children that live with one parent. I admire you.

The other side of this is the children that I see that are being neglected by their parents. Money and things are more important than teaching the children. Social life is more important than the children. We need to get our priorities in order. If you are going to have children then you must raise them in love with the attention that they need from you. Do not send them to church, take them. Show them respect as they grow and they will show you respect. Why? Because we learn more by watching parents actions than by what they say. It is like the little boy walking across the lawn in his dad's foot prints. His desire is to be like Daddy. Ask yourself are you the mother and dad that you would like to have as a parent? In today's world there are not many role models for our children to look up to. That is my reason for encouraging young couples to be that role model. It is all in God's word how to raise children. Nothing pleases me more than to see young couples, with children in tow, coming into church on Sunday. That is the Lords Day, you know.

Ky was the son that never wanted to hurt his mother or dad. If we disagreed about something and yes, we often did that. He would go to college or wherever and call me as soon as he got there and we would just talk about whatever but not about the disagreement. I could depend on that. He admired his dad. His dad was the Commanding Officer of a Marine Squadron on the base. George never wanted his children to use his rank to show any superiority to others. He wanted them to be friends with the children of the enlisted families as well as the children of the officer families. Most of their friends were children of the enlisted families. They were the ones that we met at church. Most of our friends were from Church. We never paid much attention to the rule of not fraternizing with the enlisted. I did not like that unchristlike segregation at all.

One afternoon Ky and Chad went to the Marine recreation center to play. There were several young Marines there playing pool. Ky was small in stature but enjoyed letting others know he could hold his own in a tussle. He had a lot of practice picking on Chad. One of the young men did not care for Ky taking his pool stick. So to keep from getting punched out, Ky said, "My dad is your Commanding Officer." It was awhile before we knew about this but his dad gave him a Marine Corps lecture. He often laughed about that incident. We found out later that this happened more times than we wanted to know with the boys. Ky and Chad like to play the video games in the lobby of the theater that cost a quarter to play. They would put little Shay up to asking the Marines for a quarter. Something their dad and I learned after they were grown. Our children were typical kids and I have enjoyed some of their stories after the fact.

As my children were growing up they were happy well adjusted boys. They loved life and enjoyed doing the things that boys do. George was so good with them. He taught them the basics of how to get along in this world. He taught them about electricity. They knew how to wire a house or to fix their car. They could change spark plugs or the oil in their cars before they could drive. Chad even took an engine apart and put it back together. I had seen a million motor parts strewn on a table for several weeks and him out there working on them. He finally put them all back into the car. I walked out feeling a bit sorry for him. I was never more amazed than when He got in that car, hit the starter and it started.

I feel led to put this article here, Shay wrote this to his dad on Fathers Day several years ago. It touched my heart and maybe some young person needs to write and tell a parent what they mean to them.

I Am My Fathers Son

"I am my father's son. The youngest of three boys raised in the south with a Marine from Montana as a role model. I, like many sons, surpassed my father's wisdom somewhere around sixteen. I knew for certain that I never wanted to be like my dad. I swore I'd never parent the way my father did. I swore

I'd be around more than my father was. I swore I'd Love my family more than my father did.

I am happy to say that I have gotten over the illness that touched my head as a youth. I am now an adult and a father of two. All of the work that my parents did now makes sense to me. But, speaking of Pop: I have my dad to thank for the model of the roles I play today.

Husband – When my wife looks at me softly and tells me I treat her like no other man treats a woman. I know there is at least one other. I learned from my father to hold my tongue in anger, and sometimes it's best not to say anything. I learned from my father to tell my bride "I Love You" daily and often. I learned from my father that my relationship to my wife is key to my family.

Father – I learned from my father to be consistent. To show Love. To Care. To discipline. To be disciplined. As I write this I have my 3 month old baby boy sitting in my lap. I think of the memories my father must have. The times I only know of in photographs. I understand now why my dad looks so concerned when there are problems in my life. I understand that my dad sees in me what I will see in my son in 28 years. I understand that my dad wants to shield me from trouble the same way I want to protect this small boy. I am my father's child.

Provider - My father taught me through his actions, that all (morally acceptable) work is honorable. There is no shame in digging ditches or flipping burgers. In lowering your "status" to provide for your family. I have watched my father work diligently at any job he was given. My dad said "I Love My Family" through his provision. He said it quite clearly.

Son – My father has shown me that regardless of distance the importance of cherishing the parents, siblings and family that played their roles in getting you to adulthood. In my youthful foolishness, I knew not how to cultivate the relationship with my family that I now know is so important.

Friend – I have watched throughout my life as most anyone could call upon my father for help, compassion and prayer. My dad is known and respected for being a truly genuine friend. He regularly visits whoever he may know is in the hospital. He can be called upon to fix the widow's air-conditioning. He visits in times of loss, bringing encouragement and prayer. My father has shown me to be true. To be genuine. To Love all people as Christ Loves all people. The Love of Christ knows no boundary, race, creed or financial status.

Christian – The majority of my childhood memories are centered on our being in church. I remember seeing my father have his quiet time. I heard my father pray. I saw all of my father's roles centered around one thing, his Love for Jesus Christ. I pray to be as faithful. I have a living example of the Love of Christ in my Dad.

Hearing my fathers profession and from where he was raised, even the outsider can picture a coarse, rugged man. This is quite the contrary to what my father is. Despite his upbringing, dad came to Christ and through circumstances that only God can orchestrate came from the Great Northwest to a small town in Mississippi to find and wed my Mom.

My father gave control of his marriage, his parenting and all of his roles to Jesus Christ. My childhood memories are seasoned with family vacations and play and every Sunday morning my father fixing breakfast for us to get up and out the door to get to church and learn about Jesus Christ.

I thank my Heavenly Father for my Earthly Father. Who has traveled his path well and focused his life and goals on Christ. In doing so he pointed his family in the same direction. Molding his boys to follow in his footsteps. His goal was not for us to be famous or rich. His goal was for us to grow to know Christ and in turn show His Love to our Wives and Children and anyone that God might put in our path.

My dad, I believe, would be completely content with no thanks. He has never done anything with his own reward in mind.

I take this time now as an adult, with a bride and two children of my own, having had an opportunity to see successes and failures in all of my given roles. To say THANK YOU to my role model. My Father. My Dad. My Pop.

I Love You Dad. And I want you to know that I am glad when people compare me to you, and when I hear your words come out of my mouth. I want to Live and Love and Serve Christ in the way that you modeled.

I am proud to be and had the opportunity to be Shay Berthelson, your Son,

I Love You
Thank You "

Proverbs 29:23 *A man's pride shall bring him low: but honour shall uphold the humble in spirit.*

My Soldier Chad

Proverbs 1:33 *But whoso hearkeneth unto me shall dwell safely, and shall be quiet from fear of evil.*

My sons never were sorry they were in a military family. They enjoyed the experiences that they were exposed to by moving from one base to another. Living in Okinawa for a year was a wonderful experience for all of the family. As a mother I never encouraged them to go into the military. I did not want them to go to war. The discipline that is learned in the military is a wonderful asset to take anyone through life.

Chad went to college at Mississippi State on a scholarship. He studied hard and was a good son.

He called me to tell me he had joined the Army National Guard. I was not one bit excited about that but he had joined so I just complimented him. What else can a mother do?

He married his high school sweetheart, Brenda, before he graduated. Brenda also went to State and got a Master degree in Education quickly. She was a very determined young lady. After Brenda received her degree she taught school.

Chad had to go to his weekend guard duty but that was ok with me but when the Desert Storm happened, I got the call that I did not want to hear. "Mom, I have been called up." That was this Mama's nightmare of the service. He went to Texas and was out in the woods most of the time when Brenda decided she wanted to go to see him. Shay, her dear brother-in-law, did not want her to go alone so he offered to go with her. Shay is like a brother to Brenda since he was just a kid when she began to date Chad.

They are on their way to Texas when Brenda finally decided to let him drive. They were riding along and suddenly Shay grabbed his chest and fell over the steering wheel. Oh my goodness! Brenda almost panicked as she thought he had a heart attack. Well, he was playing a joke and being the jokester that he is, he thought it was very funny. Needless to say, Brenda did not.

When they arrive in Texas, late at night, Shay goes into a barracks to see if he could find his brother. Chad had been in the field for weeks and this happened to be the first night he was able to come into the barracks to get a hot shower. As he was walking down the hall with a towel around him, he begins to squint because there is a guy coming toward him that looked like Shay. He though he must be hallucinating since he didn't know Brenda was coming to town, much less Shay. Well, it was Shay. This is a very typical story of our Shay. He appears when you least expect him. He enjoys scaring the daylights out of his mother.

Chad had gotten as far as California on his way to Saudi Arabia when the war ended. Only by his grace did this happen. I do not think this mother would have handled that very well, but it gave me a lot of compassion for mothers whose sons or daughters were there. When we pray we should never forget the military families. It is a daily heartache when one of their loved ones is not home. George and I were very proud of Chad having the desire to serve his country but it was not what we would have chosen because as parents we wanted to protect our children from all harm. No parent can do that.

Children are going to grow up and we must let them "fly". So many parents never really let their children go. It is not good to hang on so tight that they cannot become what God would have them to be. Many young people cannot find their purpose because they are afraid they will not please their parents, or maybe even hurt their feelings. That string is tied too tight parents, for their sake let them grow up. You made decisions that most likely your parents didn't like but you made them anyway. That is what our children should be able to do. If they make a mistake they will learn from it as you and I did. Let go of the rope that is tied to you. How can God use them if they have to please mom and dad in every decision they make?

Chad knew he did not have to call and ask us if he could join the National Guard. He knew we would accept his decision. One of the things that I remember about Chad is that he sent me his military check during his summer at boot camp. Money was short in this household. He never said a word about that. He was just helping his mom and dad.

Matthew 9:37-38 *Then he said unto his disciples, The harvest is plenteous, but the laborers are few; Pray ye therefore the Lord of the harvest, that he will send forth laborers into his harvest.*

Chapter 5

Now To My Sadness

Isaiah 41:10 *Fear thou not; for I am with thee; be not dismayed; for I am thy God: I will strengthen thee; yea, I will help thee; yea, I will uphold thee with the right hand of they righteousness.*

I have told you how close I was to my parents. I loved them and wanted to please them. They taught me how to become a good person and that was my desire. I loved people and treated them so they would know it.

We were living on the base at Beaufort, South Carolina. I was teaching at Laurel Bay Elementary. I was filling in for a teacher that was on maternity leave. I would not take a full time position because I wanted to be home for my boys. If they were sick I wanted to be their nurse. I enjoyed helping at school with the other children. Shay was only two and I wanted to take care of him. It was a wonderful time in my life, just being a wife to my wonderful husband, who I gave the name 'Flipper the Flyboy' because he loved flying and would leave on a moments notice to take his plane out.

My dear daddy died with a heart attack and we were called home for the funeral. It broke my heart to lose my daddy and to see the heartbreak of my mama. They were one in their relationship. I stayed with her a week after Daddy died and could see the grief on her face. I went home so sad knowing that Daddy had gone to be with the Lord and Mama was alone. My brother Dewey lived nearby, so did Wiley and Mary but it did not take her sadness away.

Six months after Daddy went to be with our Lord. I was teaching and the principal called me to the office. I did not think much about it other than I gave the children something to do and walked to the office. There stood George and my friend from church with this blank stare on their faces. George said it is your mother. I said, "What?", then, "she is dead". George just nodded his head. Oh what a sick lost feeling came over me. Not my mama! I was planning on going home with my family for Thanksgiving and this was November 9. This is just not happening! I was going to the Marine Corps ball the next night. I already had my beautiful white gown that had little sparkles all over it. God had changed my plans. We left as soon as the Ky and Chad were out of school to go to Brookhaven, Mississippi. It had only been six months since we were there for Daddy's funeral. Now my mother was gone. What grief when you lose your parents. Love them while you can. Let them know it.

Three weeks after my mother died, our phone rang and George answered it. I was lying on my bed crying, missing my mother. George came in and told me his sister, Joan, was dead. She lived in Montana and had four small children. She was sitting in her car, in the garage with the motor running and was asphyxiated. My Daddy's brother, my Uncle Emmett, died a week earlier. Grief hit us like a lighting bolt. Only by His grace could we get through this. I was so concerned about my little boys losing so many that they loved. Children need to know about death and they need to know about Heaven. I don't know anyone that does not want to go to heaven. There is only one way according to God's word that we are going to get there. We must ask the Lord Jesus Christ to forgive us of our sins. Ask Him to become Lord of our life and to live for Him. We need to get into a Bible teaching church and serve our Lord Jesus. I am so thankful for my church, my Christian support group from my Sunday School Class and my dear pastor, Dr. Ray Newcomb, who has never been afraid to teach God's word the way it is written.

Romans 8:28 *And we know that all things work together for good to them that love God, to them who are the called according to His purpose.*

OH YES HE DID

Jesus knew me before I was born
He told me so in His own words
Oh yes He did

He watched over me as I grew
With all the protection I needed
Provisions He made just for me
Oh yes He did

He came into this world to save my soul
Asking me to accept Him and to be bold
Oh yes He did

He went to the cross so I would not be lost
When He arose on that third day, it was for me
He became my boss
Oh Yes he did

When He said," come follow me."
He wanted me to be all that I could be
Not for my pleasure but for His
Oh yes He did

He fed five thousand with only
a small amount of bread and very few fish
Oh yes He did

He walked on water for others to believe
He told Noah to build an ark for others to see
Oh yes He did

He asked me to witness to the world
To be His voice, His hands and His feet
Oh yes He did

Will you follow this mighty God today?
Oh I hope you will.

Chapter 6

The Death of My Son

II Corinthians 1: 3-4 *Blessed be God, even the Father of our Lord Jesus Christ, the Father of mercies, and the God of all comfort; Who comforted us in all our tribulation, that we may be able to comfort them which are in any trouble, by the comfort wherewith we ourselves are comforted of God.*

Ky was as normal as any son until he went off to college. He changed and was doing things his dad and I did not approve of. One night he came down stairs and fell over my lap and said, "Mama there is something wrong with me". I cried and he cried. I asked if he would go for help and he said he would. The next day we took him to a psychiatrist he was diagnosed as having bipolar disorder, also called maniac/depression. I had never even heard the word bipolar at that time. I had no idea what was wrong with my son. From that moment, I tried to learn as much about it as I could. He would be happy and could conquer the world one day and the next be so depressed he did not want me to look at him. He suffered from the lows. One day he told me that he enjoyed the highs but he knew the lows were coming.

He would go to work and call me to tell me he had quit his job, and then two hours later he would tell me he had another job. He was a handsome, sweet and very charming young man. People liked him and he made a great first impression. Therefore he could get a job in only an hour when other young men could not get one for weeks. Quitting a job did not bother him one bit because he would go get another one. You would never know anything was wrong with him. He was very intelligent and artistic. Later I learned that most people who suffer from this dreaded disease are highly intelligent.

College was fun for Ky and he did very well with his grades. He made the presidents list often. He was in his last semester at Memphis State, came home one afternoon and went down in a wooded area not far from our home and committed suicide. When he left he told us he was going for a ride. Later that evening just before dark, George went outside to go look for him when he saw two lights coming up the road. He thought it was Ky but it was the Sheriff coming to tell us they had found him. When the deputys drove into the driveway my

George's heart sank. Then they got out and one said, "Mr. Berthelson, I am sorry." Oh, what word for a loving father to hear.

I was upstairs and had put on my gown for the evening when George appeared at the door looking so sad. I have never seen my husband so broken as when he came into the den to tell me. He was pale and all bent over. He said, "Honey, he is gone." I could not believe what he had said. George had called our pastor, Bro. Ray Newcomb before coming up to tell me. George said, "Honey you need to get dressed." It seems like as soon as I had put on a jump suit, my pastor, education direction, members of my Sunday school class and their husbands came pounding through the door. There is not much that I remember after that for at least two weeks. That is what my doctor called shock and grief. When it all began to sink in that my baby was gone, I thought I could not bear it. Only by His grace I did. Yes, precious children of ours you will always be your mama's and daddy's baby if you live to be a hundred.

Parents if your children or anyone that you know is suffering from bipolar disorder, please get them help. There is so much more help now than when Ky was diagnosed. It is talked about more now. Don't take it lightly if someone is depressed. You can help them, by listening to their problems and by getting them professional help. Learn the signs of one that is suicidal. I took the signs seriously by getting him professional help but I did not do enough. That is the way every parent or loved one will feel. I probably could have not stopped this regardless of what I did but it never leaves you for a day.

Young people don't allow yourself to get to this point. God loves you and has His wonderful purpose to fulfill in you. Don't mess that up. I believe my child is in heaven but he went before God sent for Him. I found these signs on the internet and please parents take a look at them.

What a witness our young people can be if they recognize these signs and if they should see them in their friends. Never take their talk as just talk. Most are crying out for help when they get depressed. Sometimes they may be venting about how bad their home life is or their parents are awful. Know what you can do to help someone in those cases. God will use you for His glory if only you will stay in tune with Him and listen to what He is telling you. Always remember that God places people in our life for a reason. I have so many young people that have come to talk to me, just needing someone to listen. You do not have to be a psychologist to know the signs of someone needing a friend to listen to them. Be that friend. God loves you and everyone is special in His sight so you see others through His eyes. We are no better than anyone else, just more fortunate in some cases.

Signs you should look for in loved ones and friends that possibly need help.

- **Talking About Dying** — any mention of dying, disappearing, jumping, shooting oneself, or other types of self harm.
- **Recent Loss** — through death, divorce, separation, broken relationship, loss of job, money, status, self-confidence, self-esteem, loss of religious faith, loss of interest in friends, sex, hobbies, activities previously enjoyed
- **Change in Personality** — sad, withdrawn, irritable, anxious, tired, indecisive, apathetic
- **Change in Behavior** — can't concentrate on school, work, routine tasks
- **Change in Sleep Patterns** — insomnia, often with early waking or oversleeping, nightmares
- **Change in Eating Habits** — loss of appetite and weight, or overeating
- **Fear of losing control** — going crazy, harming self or others
- **Low self esteem** — feeling worthless, shame, overwhelming guilt, self-hatred, "everyone would be better off without me"
- **No hope for the future** — believing things will never get better; that nothing will ever change

Other things to watch for- Suicidal impulses, statements, plans; giving away favorite things; previous suicide attempts, substance abuse, making out wills, arranging for the care of pets, extravagant spending, agitation, hyperactivity, restlessness or lethargy.

Author unkown

Chapter 7

My Son's Birthmother Returns

Psalms 142:3 *When my spirit was overwhelmed within me, then thou knewest my path.*

I was checking my email, as usual, and then I saw her name, Jeanne, and the subject was Ky Adam. I knew that was my precious son's birth mother that I had not heard from in forty-two years. My head fell onto the desk and I cried a stomach wrenching cry. My sister, Billie, was sitting behind me. She was recuperating at my house after being in the hospital. Billie could not imagine what was wrong. What was wrong was that in a second all the memories of that wonderful adoption to the moment I was told he was dead come flowing through my mind. I was reliving everything that was wonderful about my child plus all the hurt of the grief poured out.

I went into my bedroom and called Shay. I had to talk to someone that loved Ky as I did. I did not think it was a good idea to call George with me crying so deep and so hard. Shay later told me his first thought was Aunt Billie had died and that his dad had been killed on the way home. I scared my son half to death. He consoled me and told me it would be all right.

I had not read Jeanne's email so I went back to the computer and had this sweet wonderful note from my precious friend. She had gotten a computer and was learning how to use it. She had put in Ky Adam Berthelson and his obituary had come up. Needless, to say she was devastated. She wanted to know what had happen. I began to email her. We must have sent twenty emails back and forth that day. We connected again but my pain was so very deep. I called my brother, Wiley, who is another one that I immediately get in touch with when I am hurting. Wiley could not understand what I was saying. He called later that afternoon to console me. I had sent emails to my loved ones and friends that I felt would care. I knew no one would understand how I felt but I needed people to pray for this situation. I knew without a doubt that God was in this. He was in Jeanne and me getting together forty-two years ago so He was here now.

Jeanne is a precious person and serving our Lord Jesus faithfully. She told me about her family and her life up until that moment. I was so happy that she was living for the Lord.

Jeanne wanted to come to visit and bring her daughter Kelli. I did not hesitate to invite her to my home and for her to meet my boys and their families. These were the people that had loved Ky more than anyone could imagine.

I continued to have anxiety and fear about their coming. What would we have to talk about besides Ky? I didn't think I could talk about him and look at pictures for four days. Every thought you might imagine came into my mind. I would cry to George and Shay. I realized things were not right with me. I had to get God back into my life and to think on Him and let Him guide me. I did not tell anyone not even George my concerns about my spiritual well being. Sunday evening I came in from church thinking "okay God, we are going to talk until you show me what on earth is going on with me." What I knew I needed more than anything was for God to speak to me, let me know what to do. I needed him to assure me that He was with me through this. I got my Bible and began to search the scriptures and pray. I took the phone off the hook during the day. I was serious about God showing me what was wrong in my life. I had my retreat from Monday until Thursday afternoon and I had found no answers from God. Finally, I closed my Bible, left it on my lap and began to pray out loud. Lord just shows me what I am hanging on to? I closed my eyes and saw the letters, as clear as a bell, F E A R. Oh yes, I did! I began my gut wrenching cry all over again and said "yes, Lord". I have been afraid to let go of Ky. I have been grieving for almost thirteen years.

I began to remember the things that I had done to keep from hurting in my grief of losing Ky. Shay and Melissa had my first granddaughter. I was so proud to have a long awaited girl that I could love and spoil. Hannah had a closed tear duct in her eye. I fell apart when Shay called and told me they were going to put her to sleep and open the duct. My tiny little baby was going to be put to sleep. I would not go to the hospital. I sent George. I had no idea what I was doing other than I could not bear for my baby to be put to sleep. What if she didn't wake up? I had kept my distance to keep from hurting anymore. If I allowed myself to love Hannah like I already knew that I did, I could not bear to know that she was hurting. I was staying away from as much hurt as possible. Not consciously, but I was doing it. Chad and Brenda were having their third child and they had asked George and me to come to Pensacola and help them with Parker and Summer. Our little Heather was born. Chad called and instead of telling me we had a baby. He said, "What are you doing?" my heart just fell to my knees. Then he told me we had a baby girl, Heather, and she was having problems and would be placed in the neonatal intensive care unit. I began to remember every incident when I was called by my son that someone in their family was ill, I was a basket case until I knew all was well. I wanted to run away. I just did not know where to go. I was taking care of my grandchildren. I prayed and I called my preacher, Bro. Ray and he prayed with me. When they took Heather out of ICU and gave her to her mother. I was so relieved.

That Thursday afternoon God brought all those times back for me to remember that I was living in fear of losing someone I loved. I would worry when my children were traveling. I had not given them completely to the Lord. I thought I had but He showed me I was holding on with all my might. I began to give him my children, one by one. I cried out their names one by one. First, it was Ky. I gave him up to God that afternoon. I went through my children one by one. God I give Chad to you today. I place him in your hands. I gave Brenda, Parker, Summer and Heather to God that day. I gave Shay, Melissa, Hannah, Chase and Hope to my Father who loves them more than I do. I gave my George to Him. Knowing in my heart that I cannot imagine what I would do without him or any one of my children

My brother Wiley had been sick and I was worried about him. Don and Mary had strokes and were with their daughter Donna in Conway, Arkansas. I worried daily about them. I felt as I needed to be with all of them. That was impossible. My sister Billie had a stroke and multiple problems, so I worried about her. I am the baby of my family and I wanted to fix them. I want everyone to be happy and healthy. Only by His grace have I been shown how I have hung on to so many people that God had been saying to me for years to give them to Him. God told me clearly that Thursday that I could not do one thing about prolonging their lives. So, one by one, I cried out to God and gave them to Him. I love my family with all my heart but going through this retreat with just God and me, I learned that I cannot stop God's plan. I learned a lot by getting alone with God for those four days and searching for Him to speak to me.

Isaiah 41:13 *For I the Lord thy God will hold thy right hand, saying unto thee, Fear not; I will help thee.*

I teach Sunday school to a group of wonderful ladies in my age group. It was easy for me to tell them to give all their problems to the Lord. I had given Him many of my problems and He had taken them from me. Can a Christian hang on to the things for years that they need to give to God? Of course they can, but let me tell you it feels much better when you let go and let God handle your situation. He allowed Jeanne to come back into my life to show me that I needed to let go of my precious Ky and to give God my entire family, one day at a time. I still pray for each one a dozen times a day but God is in control. I am so thankful that He showed me what was wrong in my life.

Jeremiah 29:13 *And ye shall seek me, and find me, when ye shall search for me with all your heart.*

George and I met Shay, Melissa and the children for lunch after church the Sunday after my retreat with the Lord. I had not planned to tell them but Shay said something when he was about to leave that made his dad say, "Your mom is not the same as she was." Shay sat back down and I told he and Melissa about my week with God and I will never forget the look on that sweet face. He said, "I am so glad because I was about to call to tell Jeanne and Kelli not to come because they were killing my mother." Melissa said, "Maybe my husband can get a good nights sleep now." I had no idea I had worried my son so. Mothers, our actions affect our children whether they are three or thirty-three. I pray that my story will wake some Christian up to the fact that we are not perfect. We have people that love us and they hurt when we hurt.

I began to get excited about Jeanne and Kelli coming. They wanted to meet and visit with Chad and Shay. I wanted my boys here also. Chad lives in Huntsville, Alabama and works for the Army Corps of Engineers. He is an environmental engineer. I am not sure what that is but I know he has a master degree and is evidently good at what he does. I called him to see if he could come when Jeanne had said they would come. He could not come then since he had a project to complete but he could come a few days later. Jeanne and Kelli were fine working around his schedule. Shay has his own business, Computer Guy Services, and he could be here most of the time. They were anxious to meet these ladies also. We had seen a picture on the internet of the family and Kelli looked like Ky. I told the boys I would be fine if she didn't have his eyes. He had very distinct eyes.

They were to arrive at the airport about seven. Chad got here about six. Shay came to pick George, Chad, and me up. We left for the forty minute drive to the airport. I don't know if the boys were nervous or just trying to keep their dad and me calm but they had us laughing all the way to the airport. Here we are standing waiting for that plane. Shay kept saying, "Mama that is not them". He could sense my nervousness. After what seemed like hours but was only about 30 minutes, Shay and I looked around and no George or Chad. That was not funny to me. Shay's phone rang and it was Chad downstairs. Shay let him know to get upstairs because here comes the people that were on their flight. Shay is standing beside me and I hear "oh my goodness, there is Kelli." Jeanne is running toward me and I see my Ky coming toward me. Kellie could have been his twin. Yes, she has his eyes. She was walking like Ky and had on jeans and a pullover that I had seen on him. Now, is this God working in people's lives? You better believe it! He is real and He is real in my life, my family and Jeanne's family.

Jeanne wrote this poem the day she saw his face on the computer.

Ky's Face

Today, I gazed upon your face, mesmerized,
unable to move,
I never dreamed I'd see your face, was only by
Gods loving grace,
That face so sweet, so tender and kind, looking
back at me, as if all were fine,
But inside that face a deep sadness dwelt there,
How can others know what a soul must alone bare?
Silently depression ebbing your joy away,
deep deep inside
Who could tell the pain you had to hide
That pain so misunderstood, that you chose
to bear alone
Unless we've experienced it, to us it is not known
Everyone loved you more than words can say,
But while in your pain God carried you away,
To dwell in heaven with Him for all eternity

Jeanne Lidwell

Chapter 8

A Blessed Reunion

Psalms 34:1 *I will bless the Lord at all times; his praise shall continually be in my mouth.*

There stand two brothers that grew up with their brother Ky. Here is his half sister that looks exactly like him. A birth mother that chose to give me and my husband the child that we would love, cherish and raise to become a wonderful man. Here is a dad that is just taking it all in. What on earth are all these people thinking? One thing though, no one was at a lost for words. I think everyone was talking at once except George, who just stood calmly and watched us. We go to pick up their luggage and something special was missing. Jeanne had painted me a picture and it was not there. I could tell she and Kelli were very nervous about that. The person with the airlines promised it would be delivered to my home the next day.

I told Kelli to ride in the front with Shay. Chad sat in the middle seat with Jeanne, so George and I could sit together in the back and just breathe. That is exactly what we did since the boys were talking to the ladies. We would share a little about Memphis as we passed things we thought would be interesting. I told them to pass on restaurants since I really did not want to go to one.

We arrived home; I had cold cuts, chips and sodas for everyone to eat. Knowing that Jeanne and Kelli were probably hungry, we sat down to eat. George came downstairs on his way to Wal- Mart to buy a part for the commode upstairs. Those things happen don't they? Chad offered to ride with him. Now doesn't our God work in His own way that is best for us? That gave Shay and me an opportunity to share with Jeanne and Kelli why I had been so apprehensive about them coming. Tears were flowing down their cheeks. Kelli in all her sweetness looks at Shay and said "thank you for letting us come." I knew they needed to be with us. They wanted to know how Ky grew up.

The first day they were here, we shared pictures of Ky's growing up years. We shared stories about our wonderful Ky to these blood relatives that came thousands of miles to learn about one they had missed and loved in their hearts. It was not easy to reminisce like that, but it was necessary. Many of the stories made them laugh. Can you imagine what that was like for this birth mother and sister? Kelli was amazed at the resemblance. We have a picture of Ky when he was about 8 year's old sitting on an old wooden Indian somewhere out west. Would you believe they had one of Kelli about the same age sitting on the same Indian and you could not tell them apart? Each one had on an old cowboy hat, jeans and a tee shirt.

Ky was talented and enjoyed painting and drawing. Jeanne is very talented and loves painting. My picture is beautiful that she painted and I will forever cherish it.

Jeanne shared with us about Ky's biological father. He sounded like a very handsome man from a Greek background. He had problems similar to what Ky had. He committed suicide in the very same way that Ky did. Now that is something, isn't it?

Jeanne kept talking about my mama's cooking. You know these Southern women believe in cooking. She would cook a feast three times a day. That had left an impression on seventeen year old Jeanne. Kelli didn't know what we were talking about so we had to introduce her to a good old southern fried meal. We did just that on their second day here. We took her to Well's Kitchen in Brighton. She ate fried chicken, fried okra, black eyed peas, turnip greens and fried corn bread. She was quite the sport in trying everything. She tasted

Shay's fried green beans which was a new dish for even this Southern lady.

After our meal we knew you can not come to Memphis without going to visit Graceland. That is exactly what we did. That was a lot of laughter since my ear phones were about a half minute off of everyone else on the tour. I was looking at Vernon when they were looking at Elvis. We enjoyed the tour even for the third time for the Berthelson's. Then we had our picture taken together. That is a prize for each of us.

There was no more fear or anxiety on my part. It was all joy!

John 15:11 *These things have I spoken unto you, that my joy might remain in you, and that your joy might be full.*

I was not very hungry at dinner time since we had such a big fried lunch so I suggested we go to Sonic and get a corn dog. That was a big mistake, my boys made so much fun of me for even suggesting such a thing. So here we go for another big Southern meal at the Cracker Barrel. Kelli continues her experimenting with southern cuisine. This was another fun time for us around the table. Two families together in a oneness because of one son named Ky. This is the way I think God expects us to be when we are in oneness with Him.

The next day was Saturday and the last day here for Jeanne and Kelli. Chad and Shay's families came so Jeanne and Kelli could meet the entire Berthelson clan. Melissa, Shay's wife had come out for awhile on Friday night. She had never known Ky since she and Shay married a year and half after Ky's death. She said she always felt something missing because she did not know him. She spent some quality time with Kelli and Jeanne. Parker was the only one of my grandchildren that Ky met. He loved being an uncle. Ky, George, Shay and I went to see Parker when he was only two weeks old. Ky made him a mobile and Brenda cherishes that. Parker was two months old when Ky died.

Jeanne and Kelli enjoyed meeting all the kids and my daughter-in-laws, who are wonderful ladies. The boys and their wives took Kelli to Wal Mart. She had never been to a Wal Mart. She came back into the house smiling and saying that "Wal Mart rocks".

All the grandchildren did not know that Ky was adopted and none of them knew how he had died. Chad, Shay and their wives had to tell them before they met Jeanne and Kelli. The older ones understood this but not our two six year olds. Shay's kids decided before they arrived that Kelli was Aunt Kelli.

This reunion was wonderful but the good-bys were sad. I did not know if I will see them again but was moved by the wonderful ladies that came to visit where their loved one grew up. They met the people that loved him the most in this old world. Hopefully, we will stay in close contact by email and have more visits in the future. These things can work out just fine when we put God in the center. He was here all the time.

This is a poem that was written by Jeanne.

Ky

Like the flowers in the field
You were born,
And I found, that my heart was torn,
I could not pick you flowers, to God this one
I must yield
Father, take this flower,
He bloomed in sweetness and died in sadness deep
Take this sad flower home
In your house forever keep
You've relieved his sad silent pain
Restored his joy to forever reign
He now lives Oh Savior with you,
He's a precious flower, there are only but a few
So thank you for this flower
How he changed our lives forever,
Thank you for this flower from your field
Lord Savior

Jeanne Lidwell

Chapter 9

I Prayed for Jeanne

1 John 4:11 *Beloved, if God so loved us, we ought also to love one another.*

All the years after Jeanne left and gave me my wonderful son, I never stopped thinking about her. I prayed for her often and wondered where she was living. Who did she marry? Was she happy? Did she have other children?

I asked her questions about her life and she was so open and told me.

A couple of friends were to take her to a park the day before she left to come to Mississippi to have her baby and to give him to me. I wired her a plane ticket. When her friends arrived there was a young man in the car that she did not know. She was told his name was Dan. God works in mysterious ways. When she had Ky and went back home, Dan pursued her and he is the one that she married. They have two daughters. Dan is a wonderful Christian and they have had a good life. My prayers were answered.

Many people question whether or not our Lord Jesus is interested in our everyday life. I know He is. Every aspect of my life and Jeanne's life is all about God. How else could I get a phone number for a young lady that was in Washington? To me, one of the most amazing things about my story and Jeanne's story is that she accepted my offer to send for her. That in itself is a miracle. Most seventeen year olds would not think of leaving their security and going to live with someone they had never laid eyes on. The miracle of my baby coming to me in such a miraculous way is something that I cannot explain. I cannot imagine not having had Ky in my life. Then the fact that God in His grace allowed me to tell Jeanne about my Lord Jesus and she accepted Him and has lived for Him all these years. Jeanne and I continue to stay in close contact by email. She is supposed to be writing her story. It will be interesting to read her side of this story. I was a young bride and she was a child that God placed together for the good of a child. Thank God that she did not choose abortion. Ky was real and he was loved and his life made a huge difference in so many lives.

Isaiah 25:1 O *Lord, thou art my God; I will exalt thee, I will praise thy name: for thou hast done wonderful things!*

May the Lord Bless You

He sent you into my life to be my friend
I am so happy about that and do not know
how to begin
To tell you I care and wish you were near
For me to tell you in person that I love you
my dear
May the Lord bless you
He has showed me that you are special to Him
Therefore I need to stay in touch so together
May the Lord bless you

Today as I knelt to pray
I thought of you this very day
I asked the Lord to bless you
You are His child and He loves you so
We can be friends
May the Lord bless you

Often you are hurting or may be sad
He tells me to care for you, he cares like a dad
May the Lord bless you
On this wonderful Day!!

Chapter 10

God Used Me

Psalms 48:14 *For this God is our God for ever and ever: He will be our guide even unto death.*

God has been so faithful in using me in His service. Ever since I was a child, I have loved my Lord Jesus and wanted to serve Him. I remember the first time that I was really serious about prayer. I think I was about ten years old. My mother fainted and fell off our front porch. My dad got her back on the porch and she was just lying there. I was so scared and I remember kneeling down between the door steps and the porch and started praying out loud that God would take care of my Mama. He did and I knew it was God.

Ever since, prayer has always been a big part of my life. I pray about everything, even the wrinkles on my face. I pray for parking places when I need one. I pray for my loved ones every single day. God never hangs up on me. His line is always open for me to call on Him. When I get into my car I pray. That is some good praying time. I try to do as much thanking Him as I do asking Him for something. Oh how He has blessed me through the years.

He used a blind eye to give me a college scholarship. I was a senior citizen when He gave me the ability and opportunity to write poems and books that are distributed all over the world.

He has placed me in a worldwide prayer minister where I have the opportunity daily to witness, to counsel and to encourage people from all over the world. Some are from places that I have never even heard of. My greatest blessing is when I hear back that someone has accepted my Lord Jesus by reading the plan of salvation that I sent them.

A young man from Africa, married with children and a Christian, had an affair with another woman. He felt so guilty and needed to write to someone for advice. Our emails became phone calls. Now he has rededication his life and is serving our Lord faithfully in his church. I have received emails from CEO'S, ministers, evangelist, doctors plus a lot of everyday people that go to work and struggle to make a living. They all need someone to tell their troubles to. If they are in a church, they are not going to their pastor even though they need to. They want to remain anonymous. Some of my email friends have been writing for several years. There is a CEO of one of the world's largest companies that writes me daily. He has to go into a room and get everyone excited about the day. He is so troubled about many things. He goes into his office and emails me to pray with him about the concerns and worries that he has. There is no one he feels he can share with. I sincerely pray for him and I write a prayer to him and send Bible verses. He has become a wonderful friend that I will probably never meet in person while on this earth. There are many stories but this ministry is confidential and I would never share another person's prayer request. I am so thankful that I can sit in my home and also be a home and foreign missionary. I write several ministers from other countries almost weekly. They need encouragement. Just this week, I receive an invitation to go and speak in India. God is really going to have to pick me and take me there. My husband laughed about that thinking of me speaking to Indian people with this long Southern drawl and an interpreter trying to follow me. God does have a sense of humor. God has blessed me through this ministry more than I could ever bless someone else.

I often think of senior citizens that just give up and sit at home when they retire. God is not finished with you. If he were, He would have taken you on to Heaven. Get up and get busy in service to our Lord Jesus. I asked him after my son died to give me something I could do for him at home. Well, He answered and said, "Stay busy Sarah; there is so much to be done." I feel honored that He chose me to be in this ministry.

Psalms 71:17-18 *O God, thou hast taught me from my youth: and hitherto have I declared thy wondrous works. Now also when I am old and grey-headed, O God, forsake me not; until I have showed thy strength unto this generation, and thy power to every one that is to come.*

I have been so proud of my husband because he is as busy as can be. He teaches a men's Sunday school class and always visits the hospital if there is someone from our church there. He goes to work every day at a factory that makes dashboards, electrical panels, and wiring harnesses for boats. He is driven to keep busy and a wonderful witness for our Lord Jesus.

I teach ladies Sunday School Class and I love doing it. I do not feel that I am a great teacher but I do feel I have a great class. The ladies in my class do not gossip. They are in service for our Lord Jesus. We love the Lord and each other. We are striving to have the most Christ-centered class we can possibly have. We know that if we let our guard down, then Satan will use that to cause conflict in our class. We work at not allowing that to happen.

The first book that I wrote, <u>He Guides My Path</u>, was written twenty-seven years before it was published. I was at Ridgecrest, North Carolina when a wonderful man with a publishing company told me I had a story to tell. He encouraged me to write to him when I got home. I did and he wanted me to write my story about the adoption of my son since it was done in such a miraculous way.

My husband received orders to Okinawa when we came home. I decided the boys and I were going with him. Well, we did and I began writing my story. No one knew that I was writing it except Chad. He came home from school and asked me what I was doing and I told him I was writing a book. He said, "What is the name of it?" I wrote across that old notebook, "He Guides My Path." When we got back to the United States, I gave the manuscript to my husband and asked him to destroy it. I did not want to embarrass my son that was adopted. He was very sensitive and did not like calling attention to himself. After his death, my husband got the manuscript off the top of our china cabinet. I added three chapters and then my first book was published, in God's timing and his divine providence. Then I was asked to write another one and that one is Just Jesus. Chad read it and advised me to put the plan of salvation in it. I did. Many have read it and accepted our Lord Jesus. That is how our God works things out. He waited until I was a senior citizen before having me write books. So what is he asking you as a senior to do? I believe there is much more for us to do than to be entertained.

Jeremiah 33:3 *Call unto me, and I will answer thee, and show thee great and mighty things, which thou knowest not.*

I have claimed that verse so many times but I never thought once that I would be writing books. My blessing is when someone emails, calls or tells me they have enjoyed reading the books. May you also be blessed.

Chapter 11

The Fruits in Our Life

G od is good all the time and He desires the best for each of His children. I want the best for you also and for you to enjoy the fruits of the Spirit.

Galatians 5:22-23 *But the fruit of the Spirit is love, joy, peace, longsuffering, gentleness, goodness, faith, meekness, temperance: against such there is no law.*

We are searching for love in all the wrong places today. Our first love should be our Lord Jesus Christ. If He is, then you will not have to get on the internet or go to a bar room to search for love. Love should begin in the home with our spouse and our children. Children should feel love. How can they relate to a loving heavenly Father if they do not have one at home. We need to cherish our children. They need to see their dad being a loving husband and the mother a supportive, happy wife. Happiness is contagious. That is what I remember wanting my sons to see in their home. Not the fact their dad was a big, bad Marine pilot but a man that loved them and taught them the love of our Lord.

Joy is that feeling of contentment in our lives. God is first, our loved ones second and friends are next. Our life becomes joyful as we place things in the right order.

Isaiah 55:12 *For ye shall go out with joy, and be led forth with peace: the mountains and the hills shall break forth before you into singing, and the trees of the field shall clap their hands.*

Isn't it exciting when you see someone that is full of joy? They can see brightness in a very dull day. They can see God clearly in the fields and the streams. They go about singing with a smile on their face, even when they may be going through a storm. That is what I call joy. Oh, how I long for that kind of joy sometimes in my life. What is keeping you from having joy in your life today? Stop for a moment and think about it. What changes need to be made? Only you can answer that.

Philippians 4:7 *And the peace of God, which passeth all understanding, shall keep your hearts and minds through Christ Jesus.*

Peace is the comfort I have that comes from knowing that all is well with my soul. I love that old song, "It Is Well with My Soul". The only way that I know that all is well is when I have my heart and mind on my Lord Jesus Christ. I can't allow sin to creep in and to stay in my heart. I have learned in these years of life that Satan can get my mind but God has my heart. Satan is alive and is trying to destroy the peace of Christians. If we are serving Jesus, then Satan is going to attack. He attacks our minds through evil thoughts, depression, sadness and having us question truth.

The first thing I do each morning when I awake is pray to my Lord Jesus. Thanking Him for my home, my family, my friends, and my salvation. Oh yes, I thank God for my salvation. Without that, I am only a body walking around. I ask for blessings on the ones that I love. I pray for the ones that I know that are lost. The last thing I do before going to sleep is pray. I listen to my husband read God's word to me and to his prayer, and then I pray myself to sleep. Oh, what a wonderful God we serve! We must talk to Him and we must listen to Him. Have you had a friend that never listens to a word you say? They are always talking. That is the way we often talk to our Lord. We talk and talk and never stop to be still and listen to what He is trying to tell us. It is so important to learn to listen to Him. In fact, it is fun. I am never alone because He is here for me to talk to and to listen to. Isn't that great?

I sang a song in our old country church as a youth that meant so much to me, "Others Lord, Yes Others." I think of those words and realized how often we are so selfish. May I not be self centered, Lord.

God Be Near To Others

God as I sat here suffering from shingles
They hurt so badly that my body twinges
God be near others that suffer

Father, I have time to think of those that
are hurting
Some cannot walk, others cannot talk
Why should I whine through this pain?
What do I have to gain?
God be near others

There have been days I cried in agony
Praying with tears flowing down my cheeks
God be near others that are crying

Some are so burdened by their pain and grief
Material losses and even their vanity
God be near others

I did not ask you to take the shingles away
It was for your purpose to teach me to say
God be near others that suffer this day

Our world is in turmoil with confusion and war
Help us in our faith to soar
Lifting up others that you so adore
God be near others that have suffered more

    I believe that during our suffering that God can get our attention. He has mine. He has allowed me, through surgeries and illnesses to just think about others. I am so blessed to have one good eye. Yes, I am blind in one eye, but one of my best friends in college was totally blind. I loved him and teased him. He had such a wonderful outlook on life. Claude never complained about being blind. He was a great musician. I played pranks on him, like telling him to step up when there was not a step up. He soon learned that I was not his best seeing-eye friend. So often, we complain about the smallest things and do not praise and thank the Lord for what we do have. If you do not want to know about everyone's ailments then do not ask them how they are. They will gladly spend much of your valuable time telling you. I am sure you know someone like that. That is what long-suffering is all about. Long suffering is patience with those people. It is the opposite of short tempered. It's having a good disposition regardless of how others may be. Several years ago, I had a serious surgery. There was a growth in my throat and I began to choke. My children were in my room. I wrote the poem 'Hannah's Angel' while I was recuperating. This really happened and it touched me deeply.

Gentleness is such a wonderful virtue and something we do not see a lot of today. Have you watched TV where the man beats his wife or vise versa? How in the world can a marriage survive without gentleness on the part of both parties? I see control problems today like never before. Who controls your household? If God is the head of the home then each one should be gentle, loving and kind to the other. It makes for such a sweet home life for your children. My husband would never argue with me. Most women enjoy a good argument once in awhile. Well, I never got to experience it. My husband was a runner and if he got fed up with my bickering he just went running. He ran thousands of miles to keep from arguing. Divorce has never mentioned and we have been married forty five years. Do you get that? Stop the arguing.

Does your faith show? Our lives are a mirror to others whether you want it to be or not. Most people can read you like a book. Our faith in the Lord Jesus Christ will show as our dependability. How dependable are you and I when we are upset about something?

Temperance is self-control. This is one of the fruits of the spirit that can break a heart. Children today are not practicing self-control like they should. No one can control a child but that child. They must be taught how to do that. Why are we having so much abuse today? It is because of the lack of self control in individuals. You can say "the devil made me do it" or whatever excuse you can come up with to do whatever you please. Many young people are saying peer pressure caused them to do something that is ungodly. Well, they should learn self control and find some different friends. If our young people would value who they are, know that they are a precious thing in the sight of God, and that God has a special purpose for them, maybe they could find value in what they are. That is a difficult task if someone is telling them they are worthless.

I feel that the fruits of the spirit are very important and that all Christians should study them. They are God's gifts to be used in the way that He would have us to. He tells them about them in His word.

Hannah's Angel

Last year I had a serious surgery,
there was a growth in my throat
The doctor had told us what could happen
and it wasn't good
I gave it to the Lord after struggling
for three weeks
God, if it is my time then I am ready to go
If I cannot speak above a whisper
you already know
I did just fine and had peace of mind as
to surgery I went
The night after surgery my family was all there
I wasn't talking, just a little stare
Then my three year old granddaughter said,
'Mama look there'
'See the angel right over BeBe', the name my
grandchildren call me
She said, 'Baby where?' Hannah said, 'right there'
Pointing over my shoulder, to everyone's surprise

Later my daughter-in-law said, 'Hannah what
was the angel doing
that was over BeBe?' Hannah answered
In her little innocent voice 'He was praying'
Children in their innocence can see things
we can't see
This BeBe believes Hannah saw an angel!

Chapter 12

Reflections From Maturing

Psalm 37:25 *I have been young, now am old; yet have I not seen the righteous forsaken, nor his seed begging bread.*

B eing a kid is a found memory, even for a senior citizen. I know most young people, and certainly our children, cannot imagine us ever being young. I have to chuckle when my grandchildren tell me that I am wrinkled. Oh yes, I am. So will they be, one of these days. When I was sixteen I thought forty was ancient. Now I think forty-year-olds are babies, so therefore they need to enjoy this phase of their life. Seniors often say, "I wish I had known this when I was younger." I am not sure that I do. I have enjoyed every phase of my life. I think God intended us to enjoy life regardless of our age. I am still that teenager in my head but my body sure tells me differently. I can remember when I would call my parents and it seemed like they were constantly going to the doctor. Well that is me and George now. Our friends spend their time scheduling the next appointment, too. I have had so many opportunities to witness for my Lord Jesus in the waiting room at a doctors office. My George often smiles and tells me I must have a sign on my face that says "tell me your problems." I share Jesus with doctors, nurses or whoever will stop and talk to me. I try to do it in a way that will not turn people off. It is easy to tell someone that I prayed and God answered and I will tell them of a truth that has happened in my life. I do it a lot more at this age than I did when I was younger. As I grow older, I realize I need to do this as fast as I can. I don't have as much time left, as much time has already passed. If I put off what God has for me to do, I will be as old as Methuselah when God takes me to Heaven. Not quite, but God has given me this day to share my Lord Jesus and I am thankful that I have the opportunity to do so. It has become just as easy to share Jesus with a stranger as it is to share about my grandchildren. Who doesn't share about their grandchildren? Don't get tired of all the pictures that are stuck in your face, for you to look at someone else's grandchild. We know that not one is as cute, smart, or more talented than our own. That is a wonderful thing about being a grandparent. I think that is the reason they are called "grand." My mother use to say that "every old crow thinks hers is the blackest." That didn't make much sense to me then, but I think there is some truth in it.

Ephesians 6:1-3 *Children, obey your parents in the Lord: for this is right. Honor thy father and mother; which is the first commandment with promise: That it may be well with thee, and thou mayest live long on the earth.*

I Am Your Mother

I am your mother and so thankful that I am
You have made me proud of what you became

You are the one that is first on my mind
The one that I pray for most of the time

Thank you for showing me respect
For honoring me with your character
Loving the Lord Jesus that all can detect

I am proud to be your mother everyday of the year
Thankful for the love that I hold so dear

I love you more than life itself
Fill so blessed that God sent you
To be my child, it could not have been anyone else

I know that you were divinely made
In order for me to be blessed

I am thankful I am your mother

Chapter 13

Be Careful

2 Timothy 3:16 *All scripture is given by inspiration of God, and is profitable for doctrine, for reproof, for correction, for instruction in righteousness.*

There is a little song that I learned in vacation Bible School as a young child that still haunts me. It goes like this: "Oh, be careful little eyes, what you see. Oh, be careful little ears, what you hear. Oh, be careful little mouth, what you say. Oh, be careful little hands, what you do. Oh, be careful, little feet, where you go." In my heart I know exactly what that little song is teaching me. Yet, I look at things that I should not see. We never get those things out of our head. It is like when I see a snake. I cannot stand snakes. I do not like to see one on TV and if I see a snake I scream. So that is not good for me to see. I have listened to gossip and I know that I should not because it stigmatizes the person being discussed in my mind. It is not good to listen to someone tell you something negative about a person, for once it enters your brain, it is in there for keeps. I have also gotten into some messy situations with my hands. I remember going fishing with my daddy and my brother, Dewey, but before we fished we had to go dig up worms from under the ground. I did not like digging nor did I like touching the worms but it was necessary to catch a fish. What do you allow your eyes to see, your ears to hear, your hands to touch? Stop for a moment and make a check list of whether it is what Jesus would have you do. You know, He is watching everything. So be very careful. Would you be happy to know that your children were doing the same that you are? Young people, would you be pleased for your parents to know what you are doing?

I think my mouth should be godly and it is not always godly. When we repeat something that we do not know to be true, it is like the old game of gossip. It never turns out right. I often tell my Sunday school ladies to get it right before repeating news. It can be a prayer request, but it should be told correctly. Sometimes we lie. Now, don't get too pious on me here. Yes, we Christian lie. I have had a telemarketer call and ask for my husband and I told them that he was not here. That was a lie. Many people tells us things to make a point, a preacher may call it a parable. If it is not the truth then it is a lie. We need to watch our tongue. I feel that watching our tongue is one of our most effective witnessing tools that God gave us. We do not fool people. Many people have ended up in court for telling a lie. What does Jesus think of lying? Our mouth can really get us into trouble if we are not very careful in what we say, who we say it to, and how we say it.

I saved feet for last because that is what my little song does. The feet also can damage us. It is so tempting to go places that Christian should not go. There are the bar rooms. I have peaked into them and it is very dark. You have to walk in to get a drink. That is where many people become an alcoholic. That first step into an ungodly environment can get a person in deep trouble. I know young people, simply out of curiosity that has gone with a group of kids somewhere that they knew was wrong and gotten into trouble. When the ball drops and they are pulled over by the cops with drugs or alcohol it is too late to say, "That was my first time". This also applies to sex. Many of our precious young people are experimenting with sex. Some get pregnant, others get diseases but it is too late to turn back. This goes for both boys and girls. Live your life as Jesus Christ would have you to and you will not have to face these difficult times.

I hope you have been able to learn the lesson of my little song. Often when I share my testimony with a group of ladies, I have them sing this song with me. Most of them also learned it when they were a child. One young lady came up to me at a conference and told me she had forgotten that song but was going home and teach it to her children. I think that is a great idea. There is not enough good music in homes anyway.

APPENDIX A

Do You Know Jesus

Here are some facts about Salvation as I believe.

(1) KNOW WHAT GOD SAYS ABOUT SIN

Romans 3:10 *As it is written there is none righteous no not one.*

We are all sinners. I sin everyday but I ask for forgiveness and He forgives me.

Romans 3:23 *For all have sinned and come short of the glory of God.*

Why are all Sinners?

Romans 5:12 *wherefore, as by one man sin entered into the world and death by sin, and so death passed upon all men, for that all have sinned.*

(2) KNOW THE PENALTY FOR OUR SIN

Physical-spiritual-Eternal Death

Romans 6:23a *For the wages of sin is death .*

Revelations 20:15 *And whosoever was not found written in the book of life was cast in the lake of fire.*

(3) KNOW THAT JESUS CHRIST DIED TO PAY THE PENALTY FOR OUR SINS

Romans 5:8 *But God commended his love toward us, in that, while we were yet sinners, Christ died for us.*

THE DEATH OF CHRIST BRIDGES THE GAP BETWEEN MAN AND GOD

MAN'S WAY TO GOD IS THROUGH JESUS CHRIST

(4) KNOW THAT IN ONE ACT OF PRAYER TO CHRIST YOU DO;

1. **REPENT**—Luke 13:3 *I tell you nay; but except ye repent, ye shall all likewise perish.*
2. **BELIEVE**— ACTS 16:31 *And they said, Believe on the Lord Jesus Christ and thou shalt be saved*
3. **RECEIVE**—Romans 10:9 *That if thou shalt confess with thy mouth the Lord Jesus, and shalt believe in thine heart that God hath raised Him from the dead, thou shalt be saved.*

A TYPICAL SINNER'S PRAYER MAY BE:
Lord Jesus, I realize that I am a sinner and that I cannot save myself. Thank you for dying on the cross for my sins. Please come into my heart as my personal Lord and Savior. Thank you, Lord Jesus, for saving me. Amen

Does this express the desires of your heart?

Acceptance or Rejection of Jesus Christ is our decision. He gave us a free will.

KNOWING CHRIST IS WONDERFUL!

Acts 2:41 *Then they that gladly received his word were baptized and the same day there were added unto them about three thousand souls.*

Finding a good Bible-teaching Church and having fellowship with other believers is such a delight.

I AM A SINNER SAVED BY GRACE! Sarah

Printed in the United States
85875LV00002B/370-789/A

9 781602 667693